French Dialogues for Beginners

Book 4

Over 100 Daily Used Phrases and Short Stories to Learn French in Your Car. Have Fun and Grow Your Vocabulary with Crazy Effective Language Learning Lessons

www.LearnLikeNatives.com

www.LearnLikeNatives.com

© Copyright 2020

By Learn Like A Native

ALL RIGHTS RESERVED

No part of this book may be reproduced, stored in a retrieval system, or transmitted in any form or by any means, without the prior written permission of the publisher.

www.LearnLikeNatives.com

TABLE OF CONTENT

INTRODUCTION	5
CHAPTER 1 The Driver's License / question words	17
Translation of the Story	33
The Driver's License	33
CHAPTER 2 At the Travel Agency / likes and dislikes	45
Translation of the Story	63
At the Travel Agency	63
CHAPTER 3 Valentine's Day in Paris / prepositions	76
Translation of the Story	93
Valentine's Day in Paris	93
CONCLUSION	104
About the Author	110

www.LearnLikeNatives.com

www.LearnLikeNatives.com

INTRODUCTION

Before we dive into some French, I want to congratulate you, whether you're just beginning, continuing, or resuming your language learning journey. Here at Learn Like a Native, we understand the determination it takes to pick up a new language and after reading this book, you'll be another step closer to achieving your language goals. As a thank you for learning with us, we are giving you free access to our 'Speak Like a Native' eBook. It's packed full of practical advice and insider tips on how to make language learning quick, easy, and most importantly, enjoyable. Head over to LearnLikeNatives.com to access your free guide and peruse our huge selection of language learning resources.

Learning a new language is a bit like cooking—you need several different ingredients and the right technique, but the end result is sure to be delicious. We created this book of short stories for learning French because language is alive. Language is about the senses—hearing, tasting the words on your tongue, and touching another culture up close. Learning a language in a classroom is a fine place to start, but it's not a complete introduction to a language.

In this book, you'll find a language come to life. These short stories are miniature immersions into the French language, at a level that is perfect for beginners. This book is not a lecture on grammar. It's not an endless vocabulary list. This book is the closest you can come to a language immersion without leaving the country. In the stories within, you will see people speaking to each other, going through daily life situations, and using the most common, helpful words and phrases in language.

You are holding the key to bringing your French studies to life.

Made for Beginners

We made this book with beginners in mind. You'll find that the language is simple, but not boring. Most of the book is in the present tense, so you will be able to focus on dialogues, root verbs, and understand and find patterns in subject-verb agreement.

This is not "just" a translated book. While reading novels and short stories translated into French is a wonderful thing, beginners (and even novices) often run into difficulty. Literary licenses and complex sentence structure can make reading in your second language truly difficult—not to mention BORING. That's why French Short Stories for Beginners is the perfect book to pick up. The stories are simple, but not infantile. They were not written for children, but the language is simple so that beginners can pick it up.

The Benefits of Learning a Second Language

If you have picked up this book, it's likely that you are already aware of the many benefits of learning a second language. Besides just being fun, knowing more than one language opens up a whole new world to you. You will be able to communicate with a much larger chunk of the world. Opportunities in the workforce will open up, and maybe even your day-to-day work will be improved. Improved communication can also help you expand your business. And from a neurological perspective, learning a second language is like taking your daily vitamins and eating well, for your brain!

www.LearnLikeNatives.com

How To Use The Book

The chapters of this book all follow the same structure:

- A short story with several dialogs
- A summary in French
- A list of important words and phrases and their English translation
- Questions to test your understanding
- Answers to check if you were right
- The English translation of the story to clear every doubt

You may use this book however is comfortable for you, but we have a few recommendations for getting the most out of the experience. Try these tips and if they work for you, you can use them on every chapter throughout the book.

www.LearnLikeNatives.com

1) Start by reading the story all the way through. Don't stop or get hung up on any particular words or phrases. See how much of the plot you can understand in this way. We think you'll get a lot more of it than you may expect, but it is completely normal not to understand everything in the story. You are learning a new language, and that takes time.

2) Read the summary in French. See if it matches what you have understood of the plot.

3) Read the story through again, slower this time. See if you can pick up the meaning of any words or phrases you don't understand by using context clues and the information from the summary.

4) Test yourself! Try to answer the five comprehension questions that come at the end of each story. Write your answers

down, and then check them against the answer key. How did you do? If you didn't get them all, no worries!

5) Look over the vocabulary list that accompanies the chapter. Are any of these the words you did not understand? Did you already know the meaning of some of them from your reading?

6) Now go through the story once more. Pay attention this time to the words and phrases you haven't understand. If you'd like, take the time to look them up to expand your meaning of the story. Every time you read over the story, you'll understand more and more.

7) Move on to the next chapter when you are ready.

www.LearnLikeNatives.com

Read and Listen

The audio version is the best way to experience this book, as you will hear a native French speaker tell you each story. You will become accustomed to their accent as you listen along, a huge plus for when you want to apply your new language skills in the real world.

If this has ignited your language learning passion and you are keen to find out what other resources are available, go to LearnLikeNatives.com, where you can access our vast range of free learning materials. Don't know where to begin? An excellent place to start is our 'Speak Like a Native' free eBook, full of practical advice and insider tips on how to make language learning quick, easy, and most importantly, enjoyable.

www.LearnLikeNatives.com

And remember, small steps add up to great advancements! No moment is better to begin learning than the present.

www.LearnLikeNatives.com

FREE BOOK!

Get the *FREE BOOK* that reveals the secrets path to learn any language fast, and without leaving your country.

Discover:

- The **language 5 golden rules** to master languages at will

- Proven **mind training techniques** to revolutionize your learning

- A complete step-by-step guide to **conquering any language**

www.LearnLikeNatives.com

www.LearnLikeNatives.com

www.LearnLikeNatives.com

CHAPTER 1
The Driver's License / question words

HISTOIRE

Wayne vit dans une ville. Wayne a quarante ans. Il conduit habituellement sa voiture pour se rendre au travail. Wayne est en retard au travail aujourd'hui. Wayne roule de plus en plus vite. Il roule au-dessus de la limitation de vitesse. Il doit se rendre au travail à l'heure. Aujourd'hui, il a une réunion importante.

Wayne entend un bruit. Il regarde derrière lui. Il y a une voiture de police derrière lui. « Oh, non, pense-t-il. Je vais plutôt vite. » Il arrête la voiture.

La voiture de police s'arrête aussi. Un policier sort. Il marche jusqu'à la voiture de Wayne.

« Bonjour, » dit le policier.

« Bonjour, monsieur », dit Wayne.

« **Pourquoi** pensez-vous que je vous ai arrêté ? » demande le policier.

« Je ne sais pas. **Quelle** loi enfreins-je? » demande Wayne.

« Vous allez beaucoup trop vite », dit le policier.

« **Combien de** kilomètres à l'heure suis-je au-dessus de la limitation de vitesse? » demande Wayne.

« Assez, dit le policier. **Où** allez-vous si vite? »

« Au travail », dit Wayne.

« Montrez-moi votre permis de conduire », dit l'agent. Wayne sort son portefeuille. Il l'ouvre. Il retire son permis de conduire. Il le donne à l'officier de police.

« Ce permis est expiré », dit l'agent. « Vous avez de gros problèmes. » L'agent dit à Wayne qu'il ne peut pas conduire avec un permis expiré. Wayne doit obtenir un nouveau permis. Wayne est d'accord. L'agent lui dit qu'il ne peut pas aller au travail en voiture aujourd'hui. Wayne doit vivre sans voiture.

Wayne doit arrêter de conduire sa voiture. Maintenant, il va travailler autrement. Il peut choisir entre le train ou l'autobus. Parfois, il fait du vélo. S'il est en retard, il prend un taxi. Aujourd'hui, il est encore en retard.

Wayne arrive au bureau.

« Bonjour, Wayne », dit son collègue, Xavier. « **Comment** êtes-vous venu ici? Votre permis est expiré, n'est-ce pas? »

« Oui, c'est le cas, dit Wayne. Aujourd'hui, je suis venu en taxi. **À quelle distance** se trouve votre maison? » Xavier se rend habituellement au travail à pied.

« Ma maison est à un kilomètre, dit Xavier. **Combien de temps** faut-il pour arriver en taxi? »

« Oh, environ 20 minutes », dit Wayne.

« Pas mal, dit Xavier. Et **combien coûte** le taxi? »

« Environ vingt dollars », dit Wayne.

« Oh, c'est un peu cher, dit Xavier. Quelle compagnie de taxi est-ce?

« Birmingham Taxi », dit Wayne. « Pourquoi êtes-vous si intéressé? »

« Ma famille possède une compagnie de taxi, dit Xavier. Mon frère la dirige. »

« Super, dit Wayne. Est-ce que je peux avoir un trajet gratuit? » Ils rient tous les deux. Wayne plaisante. Mais il doit résoudre son problème. Il ne peut pas payer un taxi tous les jours. Il décide que demain il va aura son nouveau permi.

www.LearnLikeNatives.com

Le lendemain, Wayne prend l'autobus pour se rendre au Bureau des Permis, le département des véhicules automobiles, où les gens obtiennent leur permis de conduire. Il sort de sa voiture. Il y a la queue dehors. Beaucoup de gens doivent obtenir leur permis. Les employés du bureau sont lents. Il fait la queue. Après une heure, il est à l'intérieur de l'immeuble. Il y a une autre file d'attente. Il attend.

« **Qui** est le prochain? » demande la femme.

« Moi », dit Wayne.

« Eh bien, venez! » dit-elle. Elle est impatiente. « De quoi avez-vous besoin? »

« Je dois renouveler mon permis », dit Wayne.

« Donnez-moi votre ancienne carte », dit-elle.

« Je ne l'ai pas, » dit Wayne. Elle le fixe. Elle semble en colère.

« **Pourquoi ne** l'avez-vous **pas** ? » demande-t-elle.

« Je ne le trouve pas », dit Wayne.

« **Avec qui est-ce que je parle**? » demande-t-elle.

« Que voulez-vous dire? » demande Wayne. Il est confus.

« Bon, petit malin, dis-moi ton prénom et ton nom », dit-elle. Wayne lui dit. « **Quel âge** avez-vous? » demande-t-elle.

« **Pour quoi**? » demande Wayne.

« Je dois confirmer votre date de naissance, dit-elle. **Quand** êtes-vous né? »

Wayne lui dit. Elle regarde son ordinateur. Elle prend beaucoup de temps. Elle secoue la tête.

« Je ne peux pas vous trouver, dit-elle. Il y a un problème avec le système aujourd'hui. Revenez demain. »

« Je ne peux pas », dit Wayne.

« Si vous voulez votre permis aujourd'hui, vous devrez passer l'examen de conduite », dit-elle.

« **Pourquoi**? » demande Wayne.

www.LearnLikeNatives.com

« L'ordinateur dit que vous n'avez pas de permis », dit-elle. Wayne a besoin de son permis aujourd'hui. Il se rend dans l'autre file d'attente. Il passera son permis de conduire. Facile, pense-t-il. Il sait conduire. Tous les autres sont des adolescents. Il est le plus âgé dans cette file.

« **À qui** le tour ? » demande un grand homme avec un costume marron.

« Le mien », dit Wayne. Il suit le grand homme jusqu'à sa voiture. Ils montent dans la voiture. Wayne essaie de se souvenir de tout ce qu'on fait lors d'un examen de conduite. Il vérifie les rétroviseurs. Il met sa ceinture de sécurité. Il voit l'examinateur écrire sur un bloc-notes.

« D'accord, allons-y », explique l'examinateur.

Wayne sort de l'emplacement de stationnement en faisant attention. Il conduit lentement. Il utilise son clignotant. Il prend la route et roule sous la limite de vitesse. L'examinateur le dirige à travers la ville. Wayne s'assure de s'arrêter aux feux orange et d'utiliser son clignotant. Wayne fait du bon travail.

Wayne pense qu'il a réussi. L'examinateur lui dit de retourner au Bureau. Cependant, l'examinateur lui dit d'arrêter.

« Maintenant, vous devez vous garer en parallèle », dit l'examinateur. Wayne ne se gare jamais en parallèle. Il est nerveux. L'examinateur le dirige vers un petit espace de stationnement. Wayne gare la voiture dans l'emplacement. Il a presque fini de se garer. Mais il entend un bruit de choc. Sa voiture heurte la voiture derrière lui.

« Oh, non », dit Wayne.

« C'est un échec automatique », explique l'examinateur. « Désolé, vous avez raté votre examen de conduite. »

Wayne sort de la voiture pour laisser l'examinateur ramener la voiture au Bureau.

« Depuis **combien d'années** conduisez-vous? » demande l'examinateur.

« Vingt-quatre, dit Wayne. Il a honte. Il doit revenir demain.

RÉSUMÉ

Wayne a un permis de conduire. Il est expiré. Wayne doit prendre des taxis, des autobus et d'autres moyens de transport. Il décide de renouveler son permis. Il se rend au Bureau des

Permis pour le faire. Il attend dans une longue file d'attente et doit répondre à beaucoup de questions. Il y a un problème avec le système informatique. Wayne doit repasser l'examen de conduite. Il fait du bon travail avec l'examinateur dans la voiture. Cependant, Wayne rate son examen parce qu'il n'a pas pratiqué le stationnement en parallèle.

Liste de Vocabulaire

why	pourquoi
which	qui
how many	combien
where	où
how	comment
how far	jusqu'où
how long	combien de temps
how much	combien

www.LearnLikeNatives.com

who	qui
what	quoi
why don't	pourquoi ne pas
with whom	avec qui
how old	quel âge
what for	Pour quoi
when	quand
how come	comment se fait-il
whose	dont
how many	combien

QUESTIONS

1) Pourquoi Wayne est-il arrêté par le policier?

    a) il grille un feu rouge

    b) sa voiture est cassée

    c) il va trop vite

    d) c'est un criminel

2) Wayne a de gros ennuis avec l'agent parce que...

    a) son permis est expiré

    b) sa voiture n'est pas immatriculée

    c) il crache sur le policier

    d) il ne répond pas au policier

3) Lequel de ces moyens de transport coûte 20 $ à Wayne pour se rendre au travail?

    a) vélo

    b) autobus

    c) train

    d) taxi

4) Wayne n'apparaît pas dans le système informatique du Bureau des Permis. Pourquoi?

    a) il n'a jamais eu son permis

    b) il passe une mauvaise journée

c) il y a un problème avec le système

d) sa date d'anniversaire est fausse

.

5) Pourquoi Wayne échoue-t-il à son test?

a) c'est un nouveau conducteur

b) il se gare mal parce qu'il n'a pas pratiqué ce type de stationnement

c) il se gare mal parce que la voiture est trop grande

d) il est ivre

RÉPONSES

1) Pourquoi Wayne est-il arrêté par le policier?

c) il va trop vite

2) Wayne a de gros ennuis avec l'agent parce que...

a) son permis est expiré

3) Lequel de ces moyens de transport coûte 20 $ à Wayne pour se rendre au travail?

    d) taxi

4) Wayne n'apparaît pas dans le système informatique du Bureau de Permis. Pourquoi?

    c) il y a un problème avec le système

5) Pourquoi Wayne échoue-t-il à son test?

    b) il se gare mal parce qu'il n'a pas pratiqué ce type de stationnement

www.LearnLikeNatives.com

Translation of the Story

The Driver's License

STORY

Wayne lives in a city. Wayne is forty years old. He usually drives his car to work. Wayne is late to work today. Wayne drives faster and faster. He drives over the speed limit. He needs to get to work on time. Today he has an important meeting.

Wayne hears a sound. He looks behind him. There is a police car behind him. Oh, no, he thinks. I am going rather fast. He stops the car. The police car stops, too. A policeman gets out. He walks over to Wayne's car.

"Hello," says the police officer.

"Hello, sir," says Wayne.

"**Why** do you think I pulled you over?" asks the policeman.

"I don't know. **Which** law am I breaking?" asks Wayne.

"You are going way too fast," says the policeman.

"**How many** kilometers per hour am I over the speed limit?" asks Wayne.

"Enough," says the policeman. "**Where** are you going in such a hurry?"

"To work," says Wayne.

"Show me your driver's license," says the officer. Wayne takes out his wallet. He opens it. He pulls out his driver's license. He gives it to the police officer.

"This is expired," says the officer. "You're in big trouble." The officer tells Wayne he can't drive with an expired license. Wayne must get a new license. Wayne agrees. The officer tells him he can't drive to work today. Wayne must live without a car.

Wayne has to stop driving his car. Now he goes to work other ways. He can choose between the train or the bus. Sometimes, he rides his bike. If he is late, he takes a taxi. Today, he is late again.

Wayne arrives to the office.

"Hi, Wayne," says his colleague, Xavier. "**How** did you get here? Your license is expired, right?"

"Yes, it is," says Wayne. "Today I am in taxi. **How far** is your house from here?" Xavier usually walks to work.

"My house is a kilometer away," says Xavier. "**How long** does a taxi take to get here?"

"Oh, about twenty minutes," says Wayne.

"Not bad," says Xavier. "And **how much** does the taxi cost?"

"About twenty dollars," says Wayne.

"Oh, that is a bit expensive," says Xavier. "Which taxi company is it?

"Birmingham Taxi," says Wayne. "Why are you so interested?"

"My family owns a taxi company," says Xavier. "My brother runs it."

"Nice," says Wayne. "Can I get a free ride?" They both laugh. Wayne is kidding. But he needs to solve his problem. He can't pay for a taxi every day. He decides tomorrow he is going to get his license.

The next day, Wayne takes the bus to the DMV, the Department of Motor Vehicles. This is the building where people get their driver's license. He gets out of his car. There is a line outside. Many people have to get their license. The office is slow. He gets in the line. After an hour, he is inside the building. There is another line. He waits.

"**Who** is next?" asks the woman.

"Me," says Wayne.

"Well, come on!" she says. She is impatient. "**What** do you need?"

"I need to renew my license," says Wayne.

"Give me your old card," she says.

"I don't have it," says Wayne. She stares at him. She seems angry.

"**Why don't** you have it?" she asks.

"I can't find it," says Wayne.

"**With whom** am I speaking?" she asks.

"What do you mean?" asks Wayne. He is confused.

"Ok, smart guy, tell me your first and last name," she says. Wayne tells her.

"**How old** are you?" she asks.

"**What for**?" asks Wayne.

"I have to confirm your birth date," she says. "**When** were you born?"

Wayne tells her. She looks at her computer. She takes a long time. She shakes her head.

"I can't find you," she says. "There is a problem with the system today. Come back tomorrow."

"I can't," says Wayne.

"If you want your license today, you will have to take the driving test over," she says.

"**How come**?" asks Wayne.

"The computer says you have no license," she says. Wayne needs his license today. He goes to the other line. He will take his driver's test. Easy, he thinks. He knows how to drive. All the other people are teenagers. He is the oldest in this line.

"**Whose** turn is it?" asks a big man with a brown suit.

"Mine," says Wayne. He follows the big man to his car. They get in the car. Wayne tries to remember everything you do in a driver's test. He checks the mirrors. He puts on his seatbelt. He sees the examiner writing on a notepad.

"Okay, let's go," says the examiner.

Wayne carefully backs out of the parking space. He drives slowly. He uses his turn signal. He gets on the road and drives under the speed limit. The examiner directs him through the town. Wayne makes sure to stop at yellow lights and to use his blinker. Wayne does a good job.

Wayne thinks he passes. The examiner directs him back to the DMV. However, the examiner tells him to stop.

"Now you must parallel park," says the examiner. Wayne never parallel parks. He is nervous. The examiner directs him to a tiny parking space. Wayne turns the car into the space. He is almost finished parking. But then he hears a 'ding' sound. His car hits the car behind him.

"Oh, no," says Wayne.

"That is an automatic fail," says the examiner. "Sorry, you fail your driver's test."

Wayne gets out of the car to let the examiner drive the car back to the office.

"**How many** years have you been driving?" asks the examiner.

"Twenty-four," says Wayne. He is ashamed. He has to come back tomorrow.

www.LearnLikeNatives.com

www.LearnLikeNatives.com

CHAPTER 2
At the Travel Agency / likes and dislikes

HISTOIRE

Yolanda et Zelda sont sœurs. Elles ont une vie très remplie. Elles vivent toutes les deux à New York. Yolanda est coiffeuse pour les célébrités. Zelda est avocate et a deux enfants. Elles sont tellement occupées que parfois elles ne se voient pas pendant des mois.

Yolanda a une idée un jour. Elle appelle Zelda.

« Zelda, ma chérie ! Comment vas-tu ? demande-t-elle.

www.LearnLikeNatives.com

« Bien, sœurette, dit Zelda. Comment ça va? »

« Super! J'ai eu une idée merveilleuse, dit Yolanda. **Nous devrions** faire un voyage ensemble! »

« Quelle excellente idée, dit Zelda. **Je l'adore**! Où aller? »

« Je ne sais pas, n'importe où, dit Yolanda. Partout! **J'aimerais** aller n'importe où avec toi! »

« Allons à l'agence de voyages demain, dit Zelda. Ils peuvent nous aider. »

Les sœurs se rencontrent le lendemain. Zelda apporte des pages de recherche sur les vacances. Les pages parlent de différents types de voyages. Il y a le tourisme récréatif, qui consiste à se détendre et s'amuser à la plage. Il y a le tourisme culturel qui consiste à visiter des musées pour en apprendre davantage sur l'histoire et l'art. Le tourisme d'aventure est pour les gens qui **adorent** explorer des endroits éloignés et les activités extrêmes. L'écotourisme, c'est aller dans des lieux naturels.

Yolanda lit les journaux. Le tourisme sanitaire consiste à prendre soin de votre corps et de votre esprit en visitant des endroits comme des stations thermales. Le tourisme religieux est un voyage qui consiste à célébrer des événements religieux ou à visiter des lieux religieux importants.

« Il y a tellement de types de voyages », dit Yolanda.

« Oui, dit Zelda. **J'aime** voyager pour une raison. Je ne peux pas rester allongée sur la plage, ne rien faire. » Yolanda aime la plage. Elle aime ne rien faire en vacances. Elle ne dit rien.

Les sœurs arrivent à l'agence de voyages. L'agent de voyages est une femme. Elle a l'air gentille. Yolanda et Zelda s'assoient avec elle.

« Comment puis-je vous aider? » demande l'agent.

« Nous aimerions faire un voyage », dit Yolanda.

« Quel genre de voyage? » demande l'agent.

« **Je suis folle de** culture, dit Zelda. J'aime les musées. J'aime l'art. »

« **Je préférerais** aller quelque part avec le soleil. J'adore les activités en plein air, dit Yolanda.

« Les gens voyagent pour toutes sortes de raisons », explique l'agent. « Qu'en est-il de Barcelone ? »

« Oh, je ne sais pas, dit Zelda. **Je ne supporte pas** de ne pas connaître la langue locale. »

« Nous ne parlons pas espagnol », dit Yolanda.

« Voulez-vous Paris ? » demande l'agent. « Il y a de très bons musées et restaurants. »

« Nous ne parlons pas français non plus », disent-elles.

« Et Londres ? » demande l'agent.

« Super! » dit Zelda.

« C'est tellement pluvieux! » dit Yolanda en même temps. Les sœurs se regardent.

« Tu as dit que tu t'en moquais Yoli! » dit Zelda.

« Je veux voyager avec toi, dit Yolanda. **Je ne suis pas en colère à propos de** Londres. **Je déteste** la pluie! »

« Allez, Yolanda », dit Zelda. « S'il te plaît! »

L'agent montre les photos de Londres aux femmes. Elles voient les bâtiments célèbres.

Yolanda aimerait voir Big Ben. Zelda est enthousiasmée par la Tate Modern.

« Quel genre d'hôtel aimeriez-vous? » demande l'agent.

« Nous pourrions prendre un appartement sur Airbnb », dit Yolanda.

« Non, **je déteste** rester chez les autres », dit Zelda.

« Nous avons de beaux hôtels dans le centre-ville », explique l'agent.

« Ça a l'air génial », dit Zelda.

Zelda préfère les hôtels de luxe. Elle sait que Yolanda **n'aime pas beaucoup** les hôtels de luxe. Mais Zelda ne part jamais en vacances. Elle veut que ces vacances soient parfaites. L'agent de voyages montre les photos aux sœurs. Les chambres d'hôtel sont immenses. Certaines ont une baignoire au milieu de la chambre.

« Elles sont magnifiques, dit Zelda. Cela te dérange-t-il si nous restons dans un hôtel chic, Yolanda? »

« **Pas du tout** », dit Yolanda. Zelda sait qu'elle **n'aime pas** les hôtels chics. Yolanda est triste. Zelda fait ce qu'elle veut.

« **Qu'aimeriez-vous** faire pendant votre séjour à Londres? » demande l'agent de voyages.

www.LearnLikeNatives.com

« Nous serions ravies d'aller dans tous les musées, de visiter le palais et de visiter quelques galeries d'art », explique Zelda.

« D'accord, dit l'agent de voyages. Il y a probablement assez d'activités pour remplir votre séjour à Londres. »

Yolanda ne dit rien. Les sœurs paient et quittent l'agence de voyages. Zelda est heureuse. Yolanda aimerait que les vacances soient plus son style. Elle rentre chez elle. Elle pense au voyage. Elle sourit. Elle a un plan.

Le lendemain, Yolanda retourne chez l'agent de voyages.

« Oh bonjour, Yolanda, dit l'agent. Comment puis-je vous aider? »

« **Nous voulons** changer un peu notre voyage », dit Yolanda.

« Pas de problème », dit l'agent de voyages.

« **Nous préférerions** aller dans un endroit ensoleillé », dit Yolanda.

« Bien sûr », explique l'agent de voyages. L'agent de voyages propose de nombreuses destinations différentes. Yolanda signe de nouveaux papiers. Elle donne de l'argent à l'agent pour les frais. Elle imagine Zelda en vacances. Elle sourit. Zelda **aime** les surprises.

C'est la fin de semaine. Le moment de voyager est arrivé pour Yolanda et Zelda. Les sœurs se rencontrent à l'aéroport. Elles sont excitées. Yolanda est nerveuse.

« Je t'ai apporté un café », dit-elle. Zelda prend le café.

« Merci, dit-elle. Elle prend une gorgée. Oh, mais **je déteste** le sucre dans mon café, Yoli! »

Yolanda s'excuse. Elle prend les deux cafés dans ses mains. Maintenant, elle ne peut plus porter sa valise.

Les deux sœurs passent par la sécurité. Elles attendent de monter à bord de l'avion. L'écran indique « Flight 361 to London / With Connections / British Airways ». Yolanda sourit en montant dans l'avion.

Le vol dure six heures. Yolanda et Zelda dorment. Elles se réveillent lorsque l'avion arrive à l'aéroport de Londres. L'agent de bord utilise le haut-parleur. « Si vous séjournez à Londres ou si vous avez une correspondance, veuillez vous lever et quitter l'avion. »

Zelda se lève. Yolanda ne le fait pas.

« Allez, Yolanda », dit Zelda. Yolanda ne bouge pas.

« Allons-y! » dit Zelda.

« En fait, ma sœur, dit Yolanda. Il y a un changement de plans. Nous restons dans cet avion. »

Zelda a l'air confuse.

www.LearnLikeNatives.com

L'agent de bord utilise de nouveau le haut-parleur. « Si vous voyagez jusqu'à notre prochaine destination, restez assis. Prochain arrêt : Fidji! »

RÉSUMÉ

Deux sœurs, Yolanda et Zelda, veulent faire un voyage ensemble. Elles vont voir l'agent de voyages. Elles sont très différentes. Il est difficile pour elles de se mettre d'accord sur une destination. Zelda aime planifier des vacances et voir de l'art et de la culture. Yolanda préfère aller à la plage. Enfin, elles décident où elles aimeraient aller. Mais le lendemain, Yolanda retourne voir l'agent de voyages. Elle change de destination. Zelda le découvre quand leur avion atterrit.

Liste de vocabulaire

| we should | nous devrions |
| I love | J'aime |

I would love	Je voudrais bien
I adore	J'adore
I enjoy	J'aime bien
I can't stand	Je ne supporte pas
we would like	nous voudrions
I'm crazy about	Je suis fou de
I prefer	Je préfère
I can't bear	Je ne peux pas supporter
would you like	voudriez-vous
I'm not mad about	Je ne suis pas en colère à propos de
I detest	Je déteste
I loathe	Je déteste
doesn't like	n'aime pas
very much	beaucoup

www.LearnLikeNatives.com

not at all	pas du tout
dislikes	n'aime pas
what would you like	ce que vous aimeriez
we want	nous voulons
we would rather	nous préférerions
likes	aime
I hate	Je déteste

QUESTIONS

1) Comment Yolanda et Zelda se connaissent-elles?

    a) elles sont amies

    b) elles sont sœurs

    c) elles travaillent ensemble

    d) elles sont voisines

2) Qu'est-ce que Zelda aime faire en vacances?

a) voir de l'art et de la culture

b) s'allonger sur la plage

c) se détendre

d) ne pas faire de projets

3) Laquelle des décisions suivantes Yolanda a-t-elle prises lors de la première réunion avec l'agent de voyages?

a) où aller

b) où loger

c) ce qu'il faut faire

d) aucun des éléments ci-dessus

4) Que fait Yolanda lorsqu'elle se rend une deuxième fois chez l'agent de voyages?

a) elle demande son remboursement

b) elle annule le voyage

c) elle modifie la destination

   d) elle appelle Zelda

5) Que se passe-t-il lorsque les sœurs débarquent à Londres?

   a) elles se rendent à leur hôtel

   b) elles vont dans un musée

   c) l'avion s'écrase

   d) Yolanda surprend Zelda avec une nouvelle destination

RÉPONSES

1) Comment Yolanda et Zelda se connaissent-elles?

   b) elles sont sœurs

2) Qu'est-ce que Zelda aime faire en vacances?

   a) voir de l'art et de la culture

3) Laquelle des décisions suivantes Yolanda a-t-elle prises lors de la première réunion avec l'agent de voyages?

    d) aucun des éléments ci-dessus

4) Que fait Yolanda lorsqu'elle se rend une deuxième fois chez l'agent de voyages?

    c) elle modifie la destination

5) Que se passe-t-il lorsque les sœurs débarquent à Londres?

    d) Yolanda surprend Zelda avec une nouvelle destination

www.LearnLikeNatives.com

Translation of the Story

At the Travel Agency

STORY

Yolanda and Zelda are sisters. They have very busy lives. They both live in New York City. Yolanda is a hairdresser for celebrities. Zelda is a lawyer and has two children. They are so busy, sometimes they don't see each other for months.

Yolanda has an idea one day. She calls Zelda.

"Zelda, dear! How are you?" she asks.

"Fine, sis," says Zelda. "How are you?"

"Great! I've had a marvelous idea," says Yolanda. "**We should** take a trip together!"

"What a great idea," says Zelda. "**I love** it! Where to?"

"I don't know, anywhere," says Yolanda. "Wherever! **I would love** to go anywhere with you!"

"Let's go to the travel agency tomorrow," says Zelda. "They can help."

The sisters meet the next day. Zelda brings pages of research on vacations. The pages talk about different types of tourism. There is recreational tourism, like relaxing and having fun at the beach. There's cultural tourism like sightseeing or visiting museums to learn about history and art.

Adventure tourism is for people who **adore** exploring distant places and extreme activities. Ecotourism is traveling to natural environments.

Yolanda reads the papers. Health tourism is travel to look after your body and mind by visiting places like spa resorts. Religious tourism is travel to celebrate religious events or visit important religious places.

"There are so many types of travel," says Yolanda.

"Yes," says Zelda. "**I enjoy** traveling for a reason. I can't stand lying on the beach, doing nothing." Yolanda likes the beach. She likes doing nothing on vacation. She doesn't say anything.

The sisters arrive to the travel agency. The travel agent is a woman. She seems nice. Yolanda and Zelda sit down with her.

"How can I help you?" asks the agent.

"We would like to take a trip," says Yolanda.

"What kind of trip?" asks the agent.

"**I'm crazy about** culture," says Zelda. "I love museums. I love art."

"**I would rather** go somewhere with sunshine. I love outdoor activities," says Yolanda.

"People travel for lots of reasons," says the agent. "How about Barcelona?"

"Oh, I don't know," says Zelda. "**I can't bear** not knowing the local language."

"We don't speak Spanish," says Yolanda.

"Would you like Paris?" asks the agent. "There are very good museums and restaurants."

"We don't speak French, either!" they both say.

"How about London?" asks the agent.

"Great!" says Zelda.

"So rainy!" says Yolanda at the same time. The sisters look at each other.

"You said you don't care Yoli!" says Zelda.

"I want to travel with you," says Yolanda. "**I'm not mad about** London, though. **I detest** the rain!"

"Come on, Yolanda," says Zelda. "Please!"

The agent shows the women pictures of London. They see the famous buildings. Yolanda would like to see Big Ben. Zelda is excited about the Tate Modern art museum.

"What kind of hotel would you like?" asks the agent.

"We could get an Airbnb apartment," says Yolanda.

"No, **I loathe** staying in other people's homes," says Zelda.

"We have beautiful hotels in the center of the city," says the agent.

"That sounds great," says Zelda.

Zelda prefers luxurious hotels. She knows Yolanda **doesn't like** fancy hotels **very much**. But Zelda never goes on vacation. She wants this vacation to be perfect. The travel agent shows the sisters pictures. The hotel rooms are huge. Some have a bath in the middle of the room.

"Those are gorgeous," says Zelda. "Do you mind if we stay in a fancy hotel, Yolanda?"

"**Not at all**," says Yolanda. Zelda knows she **dislikes** fancy hotels. Yolanda feels sad. Zelda does what she wants.

"What would you like to do while in London?" asks the travel agent.

"We would love to go to all the museums, visit the Palace, and visit some art galleries," says Zelda.

"Okay," says the travel agent. "That's probably enough to fill your time in London."

Yolanda doesn't say anything. The sisters pay and leave the travel agent. Zelda is happy. Yolanda wishes the vacation was more her style. She goes home. She thinks about the trip. She smiles. She has a plan.

The next day, Yolanda returns to the travel agent.

"Oh hello, Yolanda," says the agent. "How can I help you?"

"**We want** to change our trip a bit," says Yolanda.

"No problem," says the travel agent.

"**We would rather** go to somewhere sunny," says Yolanda.

"Of course," says the travel agent. The travel agent suggests many different locations. Yolanda signs some new papers. She gives the agent money for the change. She imagines Zelda on vacation. She smiles. Zelda **likes** surprises.

It is the weekend. It is time for Yolanda and Zelda's trip. The sisters meet at the airport. They are excited. Yolanda is nervous.

"I brought you coffee," she says. Zelda takes the coffee.

"Thanks," she says. She takes a sip. "Oh, but **I hate** sugar in my coffee, Yoli!"

Yolanda apologizes. She takes both coffees in her hands. Now she can't carry her suitcase.

The two sisters go through security. They wait to board the plane. The screen says "Flight 361 to London / With Connections / British Airways". Yolanda smiles as they get on the plane.

The flight lasts six hours. Yolanda and Zelda sleep. They awake as the plane pulls into the airport in London. The flight attendant uses the speaker. "If you are staying in London or have a connection, please stand and leave the plane."

Zelda stands up. Yolanda does not.

"Come on, Yolanda," says Zelda. Yolanda doesn't move.

"Let's go!" says Zelda.

"Actually, sis," says Yolanda. "There is a change of plans. We are staying on this plane."

Zelda looks confused.

The flight attendant uses the speaker again. "If you are traveling through to our next destination, remain in your seats. Next stop—Fiji!"

www.LearnLikeNatives.com

CHAPTER 3
Valentine's Day in Paris / prepositions

Charles et Dana sortent ensemble. Ils sont amoureux. Charles veut faire quelque chose de spécial pour la Saint-Valentin. Il invite Dana à Paris. Paris est appelée la ville de l'amour. Beaucoup de gens voyagent à Paris pour faire un séjour romantique avec leur partenaire. Peut-être que ce sont les films, la gastronomie, les beaux bâtiments ? Paris est toujours romantique.

Le couple arrive à Paris le 13 février. L'avion atterrit. Ils sont ravis. Charles et Dana récupèrent leurs bagages.

« Allons à l'hôtel », dit Charles.

« Comment ? » demande Dana.

« Nous pouvons prendre le train pour aller dans le centre-ville », dit Charles. **Devant** le couple se trouve un panneau qui indique la direction pour le train de l'aéroport. Ils suivent les flèches **au sol**. Ils traversent le pont suspendu, jusqu'à ce qu'ils arrivent à l'entrée du train. Ils vont au distributeur de tickets.

« Quel ticket allons-nous acheter? » demande Dana. Ils regardent tous les deux la machine.

« Je ne sais pas », dit Charles. « L'hôtel est **dans** le 7e arrondissement. » Charles devine quel billet acheter. Il l'achète et ils se rendent sur la plate-forme du train. **Au-dessus** des voies, il y a un panneau. Il indique où va chaque train. Un train s'approche. Le panneau indique « centre-ville ». Ils montent **dans** le train.

www.LearnLikeNatives.com

Lorsque le train arrive à destination, ils **descendent** du train. Ils montent les escaliers du métro. Ils sortent. La tour Eiffel se dresse **au-dessus** d'eux.

« C'est magnifique », dit Dana.

« Oui, c'est incroyable », dit Charles.

« Je veux monter **jusqu**'en haut », dit Dana.

« Sais-tu qu'ils repeignent la tour tous les sept ans? » demande Charles. « Avec 50 tonnes de peinture! »

« Je ne le savais pas », dit Dana. Charles lui parle davantage de la tour Eiffel. Elle a été construite en 1889. Elle porte le nom de Gustave Eiffel, l'architecte en charge du projet. Depuis 41 ans, c'est la plus haute structure du monde. Il y a de nombreuses répliques de la tour **dans le** monde. Il y a même une réplique grandeur nature à Tokyo.

« J'aime Paris », dit Dana.

« Allons à l'hôtel », dit Charles. Ils vont à l'hôtel à côté à pied. C'est juste **derrière** la Tour Eiffel.

Le lendemain, c'est la Saint-Valentin. Le couple a prévu un déjeuner spécial. Ils vont au restaurant Epicure. C'est l'un des restaurants les plus romantiques de la ville.

« Es-tu prête? » demande Charles.

« Oui, dit Dana. Comment y allons-nous? » Ils **sortent** de l'hôtel à pied.

« C'est juste après les Champs-Élysées, dit Charles. Ils **descendent** dans la rue. Ils marchent **vers** la rivière. C'est une belle journée. Le soleil brille. Dana remarque à quel point les bâtiments sont beaux. Ils sont tous très vieux.

« Nous devrions avoir des bâtiments comme celui-ci aux USA », dit Dana.

« Ils sont plus vieux que les USA », explique Charles. Charles et Dana marchent **le long de** la rivière. Ils se tiennent la main. Paris est une ville pour les amoureux.

Epicure n'est pas loin du quartier commerçant du centre. Ils passent devant des magasins comme Louis Vuitton et Pierre Hermé. Dana s'arrête pour regarder les vitrines. Le restaurant est **à côté de** l'une de ses boutiques préférées.

« S'il te plaît, nous pouvons entrer ? », dit-elle. Quand ils **passent** la porte d'Hermès, Charles sait qu'il est en difficulté. Il y a des sacs à main et des foulards partout. Dana devient folle. Elle prend deux foulards **d**'un présentoir. Elle saisit un sac **parmi** une pile de sacs à main.

« S'il te plaît, Charles ? » lui demande-t-elle. « Un petit souvenir de Paris ? » pense Charles. Les trois articles coûtent le même prix que le billet d'avion pour Paris. C'est la Saint-Valentin, cependant. Il dit oui. Dana prend les foulards et le sac à main à la caisse. Charles paie avec sa carte de crédit. Ils quittent le magasin. Dana est très contente.

Charles et Dana continuent dans la rue. Ils ne voient pas Epicure.

« C'est juste ici », dit Charles.

« Juste où ? » demande Dana.

« Ici, dit Charles. C'est ce que dit Google Maps. »

« Je ne le vois pas », dit Dana.

Charles appelle le restaurant depuis son téléphone portable. « Bonjour, nous ne pouvons pas trouver le restaurant », dit-il. Il écoute. La personne parle français. « Parlez-vous anglais? Non? » La personne raccroche.

« Ils ne parlent pas anglais », dit Charles.

« Il faut que ce soit ici », dit Dana. Elle repère une petite ruelle. Elle entre dans la ruelle et marche un peu.

« Voilà, dit-elle. Le restaurant se trouve dans l'allée, caché au bout.

« Dieu merci, dit Charles. Nous sommes déjà en retard! » Ils entrent dans le restaurant.

« Avez-vous une réservation? » demande le serveur.

« Oui, dit Charles. Nous sommes un peu en retard. Charles. »

« Suivez-moi, dit le serveur. Ils suivent le serveur. Ils marchent entre les tables avec des nappes blanches. Ils sont les premiers convives. Le restaurant est vide.

« C'est magnifique, dit Dana. Ils s'assoient à leur table. Il y a des fleurs fraîches. Leur table est **à côté du** feu. Un lustre doré pend au plafond.

« Que désirez-vous ? » demande le serveur.

« Le poulet aux champignons et les macaronis au foie gras et à l'artichaut », dit Charles.

« Je recommande les macaronis **avant** le poulet », dit le serveur.

« D'accord », dit Charles.

« Le poulet est servi avec une salade en accompagnement », dit le serveur.

« Parfait, dit Charles. Et s'il vous plaît, apportez-nous du champagne. » Charles fait un clin d'œil au serveur.

« Pourquoi lui as-tu fait un clin d'œil? » demande Dana.

« Je n'ai pas fait exprès! » dit Charles.

Dana et Charles sont très heureux. Le restaurant est l'un des meilleurs de Paris. Il a trois étoiles Michelin. Le serveur arrive **derrière** Charles avec les macaronis. C'est très riche. Il y a de la truffe noire sur le dessus. Ils sont d'accord, ce sont les meilleurs macaronis qu'ils n'ont jamais eu.

Le serveur pousse un chariot vers la table. Il y a deux verres, une bouteille de champagne et une boîte noire. Le serveur ouvre le vin et en verse à Charles et Dana. Il laisse la boîte noire sur la table.

« Qu'est-ce que c'est ? » demande Dana.

« Dana, veux-tu m'épouser ? » demande Charles. Il soulève le haut de la boîte noire. **En dessous** se trouve une énorme bague en diamant. Il la met sur le doigt de Dana.

« Oui! » s'écrie Dana.

Paris est vraiment la ville de l'amour.

RÉSUMÉ

Charles et Dana sont amoureux. Ils font un voyage à Paris pour la Saint-Valentin. Ils se perdent en cherchant leur hôtel. Ils ne comprennent rien au métro. Ni Charles ni Dana ne parlent français. Charles réserve un déjeuner spécial pour la Saint-Valentin. Dana ne peut pas résister aux boutiques de Paris. Ils ont du mal à trouver le restaurant.

www.LearnLikeNatives.com

Dana trouve le restaurant dans une ruelle. Au déjeuner, Charles a une surprise secrète pour Dana. Qu'est-ce que c'est ? Un gage de vrai amour. Un serveur au restaurant apporte la bague avec le champagne. Charles demande à Dana de l'épouser.

Liste de Vocabulaire

in front of	devant
beneath	sous
across	à travers
in	dans
above	ci-dessus
into	dans
off	de
above	ci-dessus
to	pour
around	autour

behind	derrière
out of	de
past	passé
down	vers le bas
toward	vers
along	le long
near	près
next to	à côté de
through	par
from	de
amongst	parmi
within	au sein
at	à
between	entre
on	sur
beside	à côté

www.LearnLikeNatives.com

before	avant
with	avec
behind	derrière
below	ci-dessous

QUESTIONS

1) Qui a eu l'idée de partir en vacances à Paris ?

    a) Charles

    b) le père de Charles

    c) l'agent de voyages

    d) Dana

2) Quelle est la première chose que Charles et Dana voient à Paris ?

    a) le Louvre

    b) les Champs-Élysées

    c) l'hôtel

d) la Tour Eiffel

3) Quelle autre ville au monde possède une Tour Eiffel grandeur nature ?

    a) New York

    b) Tokyo

    c) Dubaï

    d) Hong Kong

4) Qu'est-ce que Dana convainc Charles de faire le jour de la Saint-Valentin?

    a) rentrez chez eux

    b) aller au musée

    c) lui acheter quelque chose chez Hermes

    d) cesser de boire

.

5) Comment Charles donne-t-il la bague de fiançailles à Dana?

    a) un serveur l'apporte avec le champagne

    b) il la met dans sa glace

    c) il la prend dans sa poche

    d) il se met à genoux

RÉPONSES

1) Qui a eu l'idée de partir en vacances à Paris ?

    a) Charles

2) Quelle est la première chose que Charles et Dana voient à Paris ?

    d) la Tour Eiffel

3) Quelle autre ville au monde possède une Tour Eiffel grandeur nature ?

    b) Tokyo

4) Qu'est-ce que Dana convainc Charles de faire le jour de la Saint-Valentin?

    c) lui acheter quelque chose chez Hermes

5) Comment Charles donne-t-il la bague de fiançailles à Dana?

    a) un serveur l'apporte avec le champagne

www.LearnLikeNatives.com

Translation of the Story

Valentine's Day in Paris

STORY

Charles and Dana are boyfriend and girlfriend. They are in love. Charles wants to do something special for Valentine's Day. He invites Dana to Paris. Paris is called the city of love. Many people travel to Paris to spend romantic time with their partner. Maybe it is the movies, the food, the beautiful buildings? Paris always feels romantic.

The couple arrives to Paris on February 13. The plane lands. They are thrilled. Charles and Dana collect their baggage.

"Let's go to the hotel," says Charles.

"How?" asks Dana.

"We can take the train to the city center," says Charles. **In front of** the couple is a sign for the airport train. They follow the arrows, walking **beneath** them. They walk **across** the sky bridge, until they come to the entrance to the train. They go up to the ticket machine.

"Which ticket do we buy?" asks Dana. They both stare at the machine.

"I don't know," says Charles. "The hotel is **in** the 7th arrondissement." Charles guesses which ticket to buy. He buys it and they go to the train platform. **Above** the tracks, there is a sign. It tells where each train is going. A train approaches. The sign says 'centre-ville'. They get **into** the train.

When the train reaches the destination, they get **off** the train. They go up the metro stairs. They step outside. The Eiffel Tower stands **above** them.

"It's beautiful," says Dana.

"Yes, it's amazing," says Charles.

"I want to go **to** the top," says Dana.

"Did you know they paint the tower every seven years?" asks Charles. "With 50 tons of paint!"

"I didn't know that," says Dana. Charles tells her more about the Eiffel Tower. It was built in 1889. It is named after Gustave Eiffel, the architect in charge of the project. For 41 years, it was the tallest structure in the world. There are many replicas of the tower **around** the world. There is even a full-size replica in Tokyo.

"I love Paris," says Dana.

"Let's go to the hotel," says Charles. They walk to the nearby hotel. It is just **behind** the Eiffel Tower.

The next day is Valentine's Day. The couple has a special lunch planned. They go to the restaurant Epicure. It is one of the city's most romantic restaurants.

"Are you ready?" asks Charles.

"Yes," says Dana. "How do we get there?" They walk **out of** the hotel.

"It is just **past** the Champs-Élysées," says Charles. They walk **down** the street. They walk **toward** the river. It is a beautiful day. The sun is shining. Dana notices how beautiful the buildings are. They are all very old.

"We should have buildings like this in America," says Dana.

"They are older than America," says Charles. Charles and Dana walk **along** the river. They hold hands. Paris is a city for lovers.

Epicure is **near** the central shopping district. They pass shops like Louis Vuitton and Pierre Hermé. Dana stops to look in the windows. The restaurant is **next to** one of her favorite shops.

"Please can we go in," she says. When they go **through** the door of Hermes, Charles knows he is in trouble. Purses and scarves are everywhere. Dana goes crazy. She takes two scarves **from** a display. She grabs a bag from **amongst** a pile of purses.

"Please, Charles?" she asks him. "A little Paris souvenir?" Charles thinks. The three items cost the same as the airplane ticket to Paris. It is Valentine's Day, though. He says yes. Dana takes the scarves and the purse to the cash register. Charles pays with his credit card. They leave the shop. Dana is very content.

Charles and Dana continue down the street. They don't see Epicure.

"It is right here," says Charles.

"Right where?" asks Dana.

"Here," says Charles. "That is what Google maps says."

"I don't see it," says Dana.

Charles calls the restaurant on his cell phone. "Hello, we cannot find the restaurant," he says. He listens. The person speaks French. "Do you speak English? No?" The person hangs up.

"They don't speak English," says Charles.

"It has to be here," says Dana. She spots a small alley. She enters the alleyway and walks a bit.

"Here it is," she says. The restaurant is **within** the alleyway, hidden **at** the very end.

"Thank goodness," says Charles. "We are already late!" They enter the restaurant.

"Do you have a reservation?" asks the waiter.

"Yes," says Charles. "We are a bit late. Charles."

"Follow me," says the waiter. They follow the waiter. They walk between tables with white tablecloths. They are the first diners. The restaurant is empty.

"It's beautiful," says Dana. They sit at their table. It has fresh flowers **on** it. Their table is **beside** the fire. A golden chandelier hangs from the ceiling.

"What would you like?" asks the waiter.

"The chicken with mushrooms, and the macaroni with foie gras and artichoke," says Charles.

"I recommend the macaroni **before** the chicken," says the waiter.

"Ok," says Charles.

"The chicken is served with a side salad," says the waiter.

"Perfect," says Charles. "And please bring us some champagne." Charles winks at the waiter.

"Why did you wink at him?" asks Dana.

"I didn't mean to!" says Charles.

Dana and Charles are very happy. The restaurant is one of the best in Paris. It has three Michelin stars. The waiter comes up **behind** Charles with the macaroni. It is very rich. It has black truffle on top. They agree, it is the best macaroni they have ever had.

The waiter rolls a cart to the table. It has two glasses, a bottle of champagne, and a black box. The waiter opens the wine and pours it for Charles and Dana. He leaves the black box on the table.

"What's that?" asks Dana.

"Dana, will you marry me?" asks Charles. He lifts the top of the black box. **Below** is a huge diamond ring. He puts it on Dana's finger.

"Yes!" shouts Dana.

Paris really is the city of love.

CONCLUSION

You did it!

You finished a whole book in a brand-new language. That in and of itself is quite the accomplishment, isn't it?

Congratulate yourself on time well spent and a job well done. Now that you've finished the book, you have familiarized yourself with over 500 new vocabulary words, comprehended the heart of 3 short stories, and listened to loads of dialogue unfold, all without going anywhere!

Charlemagne said "To have another language is to possess a second soul." After immersing yourself in this book, you are broadening your horizons and opening a whole new path for yourself.

www.LearnLikeNatives.com

Have you thought about how much you know now that you did not know before? You've learned everything from how to greet and how to express your emotions to basics like colors and place words. You can tell time and ask question. All without opening a schoolbook. Instead, you've cruised through fun, interesting stories and possibly listened to them as well.

Perhaps before you weren't able to distinguish meaning when you listened to French. If you used the audiobook, we bet you can now pick out meanings and words when you hear someone speaking. Regardless, we are sure you have taken an important step to being more fluent. You are well on your way!

Best of all, you have made the essential step of distinguishing in your mind the idea that most often hinders people studying a new language. By approaching French through our short stories and dialogs, instead of formal lessons with just grammar and vocabulary, you are no longer in the 'learning' mindset. Your approach is much more similar to an osmosis, focused on speaking and using the language, which is the end goal, after all!

So, what's next?

This is just the first of five books, all packed full of short stories and dialogs, covering essential, everyday French that will ensure you master the basics. You can find the rest of the books in the series, as well as a whole host of other resources, at LearnLikeNatives.com. Simply add the book to your library to take the next step in your language learning journey. If you are ever in need of new ideas or direction, refer to our 'Speak Like a Native' eBook, available to you for free at LearnLikeNatives.com, which clearly outlines practical steps you can take to continue learning any language you choose.

www.LearnLikeNatives.com

We also encourage you to get out into the real world and practice your French. You have a leg up on most beginners, after all—instead of pure textbook learning, you have been absorbing the sound and soul of the language. Do not underestimate the foundation you have built reviewing the chapters of this book. Remember, no one feels 100% confident when they speak with a native speaker in another language.

One of the coolest things about being human is connecting with others. Communicating with someone in their own language is a wonderful gift. Knowing the language turns you into a local and opens up your world. You will see the reward of learning languages for many years to come, so keep that practice up!. Don't let your fears stop you from taking the chance to use your French. Just give it a try, and remember that you will make mistakes. However, these mistakes will teach you so much, so view every single one as a small victory! Learning is growth.

www.LearnLikeNatives.com

Don't let the quest for learning end here! There is so much you can do to continue the learning process in an organic way, like you did with this book. Add another book from Learn Like a Native to your library. Listen to French talk radio. Watch some of the great French films. Put on the latest CD from Edith Piaf. Take cooking lessons in French. Whatever you do, don't stop because every little step you take counts towards learning a new language, culture, and way of communicating.

www.LearnLikeNatives.com

www.LearnLikeNatives.com

Learn Like a Native is a revolutionary **language education brand** that is taking the linguistic world by storm. Forget boring grammar books that never get you anywhere, Learn Like a Native teaches you languages in a fast and fun way that actually works!

As an international, multichannel, language learning platform, we provide **books, audio guides and eBooks** so that you can acquire the knowledge you need, swiftly and easily.

Our **subject-based learning**, structured around real-world scenarios, builds your conversational muscle and ensures you learn the content most relevant to your requirements.
Discover our tools at ***LearnLikeNatives.com***.

When it comes to learning languages, we've got you covered!

www.ingramcontent.com/pod-product-compliance
Lightning Source LLC
Chambersburg PA
CBHW071743080526
44588CB00013B/2136